The Year in History

1937

Whitman Publishing, LLC

www.whitman.com

© 2012 Whitman Publishing, LLC

3101 Clairmont Rd., Suite G, Atlanta GA 30329

Correspondence concerning this book may be directed to the publisher at the address above, attention: The Year in History: 1937.

ISBN: 0794837271

Printed in China

Scan the QR code at left or visit us at www.whitman.com for a complete listing of collectibles-related books, supplies, and storage products.

Whitman®

Contents

Introduction

The year 1937 was in many ways a troubled one. World War II would not officially begin until 1939, but the portents were everywhere. Around the world, grim events were taking place: Stalin's "Great Purge" in Russia; the Japanese invasion of China; the bombing of Guernica during the ongoing Spanish Civil War; and especially the Nazi regime's control of Germany. At home in America, the Great Depression was still a harsh reality. Temporary economic recovery had resulted from Franklin Delano Roosevelt's New Deal, which was enacted during his first presidential term and put into practice the three tenets of relief, recovery, and reform. Roosevelt was elected to a second term by an overwhelming majority, but 1937, the first year of that term, would see a dramatic economic recession take place. In his first State of the Union address of 1937, President Roosevelt noted that the nation's most pressing concerns were improving housing conditions in both cities and rural areas; developing the social security system; addressing the problem of unemployment; and "modernizing and improving the executive branch of the government." His goal for the people of America was "peaceful advancement." Sadly, peace was growing less and less likely.

Other events seized the nation's attention in 1937. More than once that year Americans found themselves watching the skies, even in those pre–air raid times. In May, the German passenger airship *Hindenburg* met its end when it burst into flames while attempting to dock at Lakehurst, New Jersey, with 36 were killed. Newsreel footage and the radio broadcast of an eyewitness account spread the shocking news through the country, and public trust in dirigibles plummeted, putting an end to this form of transportation. Three months later, famous aviatrix Amelia Earhart set out to circumnavigate the globe in a Lockheed Model 10 Electra airplane, but did not return. Even now, questions about her disappearance abound, and there is no shortage of theories about what happened to Earhart and her navigator, Fred Noonan. On the ground, the Ohio River flood in January and February devastated a land already laid waste by the Dust Bowl.

In other ways, however, America was showing her might. A number of great feats of man-made engineering made their debuts in 1937. San Francisco's Golden Gate Bridge opened in May, becoming the suspension bridge with the longest main span and the tallest support towers, and later to be declared one of the wonders of the modern world by the American Society of Civil Engineers. The Bonneville Dam on the Columbia River in Oregon was a New Deal enterprise, and President Roosevelt himself dedicated it upon its opening in 1937. In December, the first tube of Lincoln Tunnel opened to traffic, permitting motorists to drive under the Hudson River between Manhattan, New York, and Weehawken, New Jersey. Also in this year, historic Route 66 was realigned and paved end to end, marking a milestone in the life of this important highway. Although trouble was looming in the world at large, Americans could still point with pride to national accomplishments.

Also among the things America could take pride in during this year were the New York Yankees, who won their second World Series in a row. The Yankees wouldn't stop until they had racked up an astonishing four World Series victories, with the last in 1939. Heavyweight champ Joe Louis, the "Brown Bomber," won America's heart and brought integrity back to the sport of boxing. Hollywood turned out some of its finest classic films in 1937, with screwball comedies, buoyant musicals, and stirring dramas providing welcome escape from the pressing economic and political concerns of the day. Although war was just over the horizon, and darker days were ahead, America was still an incomparable place to be in 1937.

Born on April 20 in Los Angeles, California, George Takei would grow up to be an actor, playing Mr. Sulu on the original *Star Trek* series, among other roles.

Famous People Born in

1937

T he year 1937 saw the birth of a multitude of people who would shape our world as we know it today. In every field from politics to entertainment to sports and beyond, the generation born in 1937 would have a tremendous impact on our lives.

In the field of music, 1937 gave us everyone from the distinguished classical composer Philip Glass (January 31) to classic rock-n-roll favorites like Frankie Valli (May 3) and the "Queen of Rockabilly," Wanda Jackson (October 20). Cinematic greats born that year include luminaries both onscreen and behind the scenes. Some of our finest film actors appear on the list: Vanessa Redgrave (January 30), Jack Nicholson (April 22), Morgan Freeman (June 1), and Anthony Hopkins (December 31). Other notable figures who have had an impact on movies of the modern era are producer-director Ridley Scott (November 30) and animation giant Don Bluth (September 13).

A wide range of talented writers also appears on the list. These include best-selling novelist Jackie Collins (October 4), award-winning playwright Tom Stoppard (July 3), humorist John Kennedy Toole (December 7), and gonzo journalist Hunter S. Thompson (July 18). Readers will also notice some of the people who shaped world events, from the notorious (Saddam Hussein, April 28) to the distinguished (Colin Powell, April 5; Madeleine Albright, May 15). It's clear from just a glance at this list that the year 1937 gave us many of the figures who contributed toward the world we live in today.

On May 15, Madeline Korbelová Albright is born in Prague, Czechoslovakia. She would grow up to be the first woman to be U.S. secretary of state.

January 4—Dyan Cannon, actress *(Heaven Can Wait)*

January 6—Lou Holtz, football head coach, University of South Carolina, 1999 –2004

January 11—Felix Silla, Cousin Itt *(The Addams Family)*

January 15—Margaret O'Brien, actress *(Meet Me in St. Louis)*

January 22—Joseph Wambaugh, author *(The Onion Field)*

January 24—Monte Clark, NFL head coach, Detroit Lions, 1978–1984

January 30—Boris Spassky, Russian chess grandmaster defeated by Bobby Fischer

January 30—Vanessa Redgrave, English actress *(Howards End)*

January 31—Philip Glass, composer

January 31—Suzanne Pleshette, actress *(The Birds)*

February 1—Don Everly, rock-n-roll musician (The Everly Brothers)

February 1—Garrett Morris, comedian *(Saturday Night Live)*

February 2—Tommy Smothers, comedian (The Smothers Brothers)

February 9—Robert "Bilbo" Walker Jr., blues guitarist

February 10—Roberta Flack, soul singer

February 20—Nancy Wilson, singer (Heart)

February 20—Roger Penske, race-car driver, CEO of Penske Corporation

March 2—Denny Crum, basketball head coach, University of Louisville, 1971–2001

March 20—Jerry Reed, country musician ("When You're Hot, You're Hot")

March 21—Tom Flores, NFL quarterback and later head coach, Oakland/Los Angeles Raiders

March 23—Craig Breedlove, race-car driver

March 25—Thomas Monaghan, founder, Domino's Pizza

March 26—Wayne Embry, general manager, NBA

March 30—Warren Beatty, actor and director *(Dick Tracy)*

April 5—Colin Powell, U.S. Secretary of State

April 6—Billy Dee Williams, actor *(The Empire Strikes Back)*

April 6—Merle Haggard, country musician ("Okie From Muskogee")

April 9—Marty Krofft, co-creator of *H.R. Pufnstuf* and *Land of the Lost*

April 16—George "The Animal" Steele, professional wrestler

April 19—Elinor Donahue, actress *(Father Knows Best)*

April 20—George Takei, actor *(Star Trek)*

April 22—Jack Nicholson, actor *(Chinatown)*

April 28—Saddam Hussein, president of Iraq (d. 2006)

May 3—Frankie Valli, musician

May 4—Dick Dale, surf-music guitarist (The Deltones)

Morgan Freeman, born on June 1 in Memphis, Tennessee, would go on to become an actor with numerous major films, including *Driving Miss Daisy* and *Unforgiven,* to his credit.

May 6—Rubin "Hurricane" Carter, boxer

May 8—Mike Cuellar, baseball player

May 8—Thomas Pynchon, writer *(Gravity's Rainbow)*

May 12—George Carlin, comedian (d. 2008)

May 15—Madeleine Albright, U.S. secretary of state

May 15—Trini Lopez, musician ("If I Had A Hammer")

May 16—Yvonne Craig, actress *(Batman)*

May 17—Hazel R. O'Leary, U.S. Secretary of Energy

May 24—Archie Shepp, Jazz tenor saxophonist

June 1—Colleen McCullough, author *(The Thorn Birds)*

June 1—Morgan Freeman, actor *(The Unforgiven)*

June 2—Sally Kellerman, actress

June 3—Phyllis Baker, baseball player

June 4—Freddy Fender, musician *(Before the Next Teardrop Falls)*

June 15—Waylon Jennings, country singer *("Don't Let Your Babies Grow Up to Be Cowboys")*

June 16—Erich Segal, author *(Love Story)* (d. 2010)

June 18—Del Harris, NBA head coach (Los Angeles Lakers)

June 18—Gail Godwin, author *(A Southern Family)*

June 18—Wray Carlton, football player

June 23—Niki Sullivan, guitarist (The Crickets)

June 28—Ron Luciano, baseball umpire, writer

July 2—Polly Holliday, actress *(Alice)*

July 3—Richard Petty, seven-time NASCAR Winston Cup champion

July 3—Tom Stoppard, playwright *(Rosencrantz and Guildenstern are Dead)*

July 6—Gene Chandler, R&B singer-songwriter ("the Duke of Earl")

July 6—Ned Beatty, actor *(Deliverance)*

July 9—David Hockney, English-born artist

July 12—Bill Cosby, actor and comedian

July 18—Hunter S. Thompson, author and journalist *(Fear and Loathing in Las Vegas)* (d. 2005)

July 29—Charles Schwab, founder, Charles Schwab & Co.

August 5—Herb Brooks, hockey coach, 1980 U.S. Olympic Hockey Team (d. 2003)

August 8—Dustin Hoffman, actor *(The Graduate)*

August 16—Lorraine Gary, actress *(Jaws)*

August 21—Joe Morrison, college football player and coach of the University of South Carolina Gamecocks

August 21—Robert Stone, novelist *(Dog Soldiers)*

September 2—Peter Ueberroth, commissioner of baseball

Future seven-time NASCAR champion Richard Lee Petty is born on July 2 in Level Cross, North Carolina.

September 5—William Devane, actor *(Knots Landing)*
September 7—John Phillip Law, actor *(The Russians Are Coming)*
September 11—Robert Crippen, pilot of first shuttle mission (STS-1)
September 13—Don Bluth, animator *(Fievel)*
September 17—Orlando Cepeda, baseball player
September 19—Abner Haynes, football player
October 4—Jackie Collins, English author *(Hollywood Wives)*
October 5—Barry Switzer, NFL head coach, Dallas Cowboys
October 5—Eli S. Jacobs, former owner, Baltimore Orioles
October 15—Linda Lavin, actress *(Alice)*
October 17—Zulu, actor *(Hawaii 5-O)*
October 20—Juan Marichal, nine-time All-Star San Francisco Giants pitcher
October 20—Wanda Jackson, first female rock-n-roll singer
October 27—Lara Parker, actress *(Dark Shadows)*
October 28—Lenny Wilkens, basketball player and coach
November 1—Bill Anderson ("Whisperin' Bill"), country music singer-songwriter
November 2—Earl Carroll, singer (The Cadillacs)
November 4—Loretta Swit, actress (*M*A*S*H* television series)
November 5—Harris Yulin, actor *(24)*
November 21—Marlo Thomas, actress *(That Girl)*
November 30—Ridley Scott, British film director and producer *(Alien)*
December 3—Bobby Allison, race-car driver
December 4—Max Baer Jr., actor *(The Beverly Hillbillies)*
December 7—John Kennedy Toole, author *(A Confederacy of Dunces)*
December 8—James MacArthur, actor *(Hawaii 5-O)*
December 11—Jim Harrison, author *(Legends of the Fall)*
December 17—Art Neville, singer and keyboardist (the Neville Brothers)
December 21—Jane Fonda, actress *(On Golden Pond)*
December 30—Jim Marshall, football player (Minnesota Vikings)
December 30—Noel Paul Stookey, singer (Peter, Paul and Mary)
December 31—Anthony Hopkins, Welsh actor *(The Silence of the Lambs)*

In 1937, Phillips 66 service stations like this one in Kentland, Indiana, have been in operation for 10 years. Drug stores have soda fountains and liquor is sometimes marketed as "medicine."

The **Cost** of **Living** in
1937

B y the middle of 1937, America's economic condition seemed to be rallying. Starting in 1933, the Great Depression gradually eased its clutch on the nation, and four years later wages, profits, and production had come back to the levels before the crash of 1929. But this was not to last: although historians today still disagree about the causes, the economy took a downturn, temporarily reversing the recovery and resulting in what is now called "the Downturn of 1937–1938." The economy began recovering again in mid-1938, but the employment rate would take longer to bounce back to its pre-downturn level.

The spending power of the 1937 dollar was roughly $16.00 in today's currency. An average house cost about $4,250, the equivalent of $68,000 today. A typical new car cost about $800, or $12,800 in current dollars. The average annual wage was about $1,000, which equates to $16,000 today. At an average cost of 23 cents per ticket ($3.68 in today's money), the movies were still a favorite way to escape from harsh economic realities. The figures that follow shed further light on the cost of everyday items that were part of life in 1937.

FREE
NEIGHBORHOOD CLASSES FOR ADULTS

Enroll NOW

CLASSES IN READING · WRITING · ARITHMETIC
Also ART · MUSIC · PSYCHOLOGY LANGUAGE · SOCIAL STUDIES

THE ADULT EDUCATION PROGRAM
of the CHICAGO BOARD OF EDUCATION
WITH THE COOPERATION of the WPA

A Work Projects Administration poster encourages adults to return to school.

FEDERAL ART PROJECT · WPA · ILL.

Statistics about American life in 1937:

Average annual **income**: wage, $1,010; salary, $1,750

Typical cost of a **home**: buy new, $4,250; rent, $25/month

Typical cost of a **car**: new, $800; used, $350

Cost of a gallon of **gas**: 20 cents

Cost to mail a **letter**: 3 cents

Grocery-store prices in 1937:

White bread, one loaf: 8 cents

Milk, one gallon: 50 cents

Sugar, one pound: 5 cents

Eggs, one dozen: 18 cents

Bacon, one pound: 38 cents

Peanut butter, one quart: 23 cents

Corn flakes, one box: 7 cents

Ketchup, one bottle: 9 cents

Wieners, one pound: 8 cents

Chicken, one pound: 20 cents

Hamburger meat, one pound: 12 cents

Steak, one pound: 22 cents

Catfish, one pound: 28 cents

Pork and beans, one can: 5 cents

Tomato soup, four cans: 25 cents

Potatoes, one pound: 2 cents

Lettuce, one head: 7 cents

Peas, one pound: 4 cents

Personal-care items in 1937:

Toothpaste: 30 cents

Bath soap, one bar: 6 cents

Noxzema Medicated Cream: 49 cents

Talcum powder: 13 cents

Toilet tissue, two rolls: 9 cents

Menu selections from 1937:

Hamburger steak with onion rings: 45 cents (Beverly's Grill, Oklahoma City, Oklahoma)

Corned-beef sandwich: 90 cents (Old Father and Son Restaurant, Warwick, Rhode Island)

Roast-beef sandwich with gravy: 50 cents (Steven's Hotel Restaurant, Chicago, Illinois)

Curtain rods are 9¢ each, and complete kerosene lamps, 83¢, at this hardware store in Crosby, North Dakota.

Menu selections from 1937 *(continued)***:**

Bottle of Budweiser: $1 (Cotton Club, New York City, New York)

Broiled filet of fish with parsley butter: 75 cents (Century Room, Dayton, Ohio)

"Health" sandwich (toasted whole-wheat bread, peanut butter, cream cheese and jelly): 25 cents (K&W Restaurant, Winston-Salem, North Carolina)

Beverages and side orders:

Coca-Cola: 5 cents

Milk, tea, Postum, hot chocolate, or pot of coffee: 10 cents

Chocolate nut sundae: 15 cents

Toast: dry, 10 cents; buttered, 15 cents

French-fried or julienne potatoes: 20 cents

Shrimp cocktail: 30 cents

Children's toys, typical prices in 1937:

Baby doll that cries, sleeps, drinks, and wets: 69 cents

Seven-room pulp-board dollhouse with 62 pieces of furniture: 69 cents

Clockwork toy tank that produces sparks when rolled: $1.49

Tricycle: $4.69

Football: 89 cents

Ice skates. pair: $3.39

Tinkertoys, 82-piece set: 67 cents

Chemcraft toy chemistry set: $4.48

Lionel train set, with switches and tracks: $9.95

Parcheesi game: 89c

Clothes:

Men's flannel bathrobe: $5.75

Men's long-sleeved shirt: $1.35 (monogramming, 13 cents)

Neckties: 49 cents

Ladies' stockings, one pair: 59 cents

Ladies' kidskin gloves: $1.98

Ladies' high-heeled bedroom slippers: $1.19

Luxury items:

5-lb. box of chocolates: $1.98

Ladies' watch, chrome finish: $5.95

Men's 10K gold ring with initial: $4.98

Silvertone six-tube battery-operated radio: $20.80

Kenmore vacuum cleaner: $23.95

Barbara Stanwyk is nominated for Best Actress in a Leading Role for her role in *Stella Dallas,* the 1937 film adaptation of a novel by Oliver Higgins Prouty.

Day-by-Day Calendar of
1937

I n many ways, 1937 was a troubled year for America—and the world. Political storm clouds were gathering that would lead all too soon to world war. Adolf Hitler was rising to power in Nazi Germany. The Hindenburg disaster took place. On the homefront, a nation already sunk in the Great Depression would experience a further economic downturn. To look at 1937 day by day is to see grim signs of the great conflict to come.

At the same time, however, the year was filled with remarkable events that remind us of the triumph of the human spirit even in times of adversity. Boxer Joe Louis became Heavyweight Champion and revived fans' interest in boxing while flouting the Nazi premise of race superiority. Future Nobel Prize winners were born. Benny Goodman was crowned "King of Swing," and that still-new music form was riding a wave of popularity among American youth. The technical marvel that was the Golden Gate Bridge was completed amid great celebration; at the time the longest and tallest suspension bridge in the world, it was for many a symbol of American enterprise and achievement. And this is just the beginning. Here you will find events both large and small that combined to make up the tapestry of that remarkable year—1937.

JANUARY 1

The first Cotton Bowl game is played in Dallas, Texas,
where TCU defeats Marquette University 16–6.

JANUARY 2

Actor Ross Alexander *(Captain Blood)*
commits suicide at age 29.

JANUARY 3

The first-ever science fiction convention
is held in Leeds, England.

JANUARY 4

A little more than three weeks after King Edward VIII
abdicated the throne of the United Kingdom, the woman
for whom he gave up the crown, Wallis Simpson, is featured
on the cover of *Time* magazine as "Woman of the Year."

JANUARY 5

Twenty-five Massachusetts women join 40 women
from Rhode Island in Chepachet, R.I., to open
New England's first camp for jobless women.

JANUARY 6

André Besette, Canadian
religious leader (b. 1845), dies.

JANUARY 7

In her "My Day" newspaper column, Eleanor Roosevelt
writes, "After I said goodnight to all my guests and found
out everybody's breakfast wishes, I went in to the
President's study to say goodnight. It was midnight and
I thought high time for everybody to go to bed, but I was
wrong. He was going to read his message over to his
assistants and of course, I sat right down to listen
and forgot that I had ever thought it was bed time."

JANUARY 8

Singer Shirley Bassey ("Goldfinger,"
"Diamonds Are Forever") is born.

JANUARY 9

Carmen opens at the Metropolitan Opera
in New York City, with Rosa Ponselle in the
title role. Of her performance, the Met's website
would later say, "Her dark, velvety voice is perfectly
suited to the character of Carmen: lightly flirtatious
one moment, smoldering with passion the next."

JANUARY 10

The U.S. Department of Agriculture Fish and Wildlife Service issues a press release concerning the gravely endangered California condor. It now lives only in the Santa Barbara National Forest—but there is hope, according to the FWS, that the "giant bird of California may be saved from extinction."

JANUARY 11

Days of torrential rain in the Midwest are driving the Ohio River to the highest level ever recorded, resulting in the "Great Flood of 1937," one of the country's worst natural disasters.

JANUARY 12

A plow for laying submarine cable is patented.

JANUARY 13

The U.S. government announces that Americans cannot actively participate in the Spanish Civil War.

JANUARY 14

Detective squads in New York City arrest 70 individuals in raids in an effort to break up a $50,000,000-a-year "policy racket" (numbers game). Of the 19 heads of the racket, 18 are taken during the raids.

JANUARY 15

Margaret O'Brien, who would become one of the most popular child stars in cinema history, is born. She would go on to be awarded a Juvenile Academy Award in 1944 for her appearances in *Jane Eyre* and *Meet Me in St. Louis.*

JANUARY 16

The *Saturday Evening Post*'s feature story, by Joseph P. Kennedy, is "Big Business, What Now?"

Some 2,800 Americans volunteer to serve in an international brigade fighting General Francisco Franco's troops during the Spanish Civil War. Called the Abraham Lincoln Brigade, the volunteers would be honored by this San Francisco memorial in 2008.

JANUARY 17

Richard Boleslawski, Polish film
director (b. 1889), dies of a heart attack.

JANUARY 18

Future winner of the Nobel Peace Prize (1998) John
Hume is born in Londonderry, Northern Ireland.

JANUARY 19

Aviator-engineer Howard Hughes sets a new
air record by flying from Los Angeles to New
York City in 7 hours, 28 minutes, 25 seconds.

JANUARY 20

President Roosevelt delivers his second inaugural
address. His is the first presidential inauguration to be
held on January 20, which would be the new standard.

JANUARY 21

Phoenix, Arizona, receives an inch of snowfall. Another
record-tying inch would fall on January 22, 1937.

JANUARY 22

Joseph Wambaugh Jr., future bestselling American author
known for his fictional and nonfictional accounts of crime
and detection (including *The Onion Field*), is born in Pittsburgh.

JANUARY 23

In Moscow, 17 leading Communists are tried for participating in a plot led by
Leon Trotsky to overthrow Joseph Stalin's regime and assassinate its leaders.

JANUARY 24

The first "Daytona 200" motorcycle race is held, on a 4.2-mile
beach and road course south of Daytona Beach, Florida.

JANUARY 25

Soap opera *The Guiding Light* makes its radio debut. It would move
to television in 1952 and run until 2009, making it the longest-
running broadcast program in U.S. radio and television history.

JANUARY 26

One hundred years ago on this day, the state
of Michigan was accepted into the Union.

JANUARY 27

General Motors president Alfred P. Sloan,
in a full-page advertisement in the *Flint
Journal,* declares that striking workers and
not GM are to blame for the sit-down strike
taking place in GM's Fisher Body plants.

JANUARY 28

French film *Pépé le Moko* is released in
theaters. Its American remake, *Algiers,* would
launch Charles Boyer to stardom next year.

JANUARY 29

A passenger and a Pullman porter are injured
and half a dozen other passengers are shaken
when three rear coaches of the Pennsylvania
Railroad's flier, *The Constitution,* are derailed.

JANUARY 30

Speaking to the Reichstag in Berlin, Adolf Hitler
says, "The National Socialist program replaces
the liberalistic conception of the individual
by the conception of a people bound
by their blood to the soil. Of all the tasks
with which we are confronted, it is the grandest
and most sacred task of man to preserve his race."

JANUARY 31

A blizzard in the high Sierras isolates more than 5,000 people in the mining communities of Grass Valley and Nevada City. Snowdrifts are as much as 12 feet high.

On January 18, 1937, Howard Hughes sets a transcontinental airspeed record, flying from Los Angeles to Newark, New Jersey, in 7 hours, 28 minutes, 25 seconds.

FEBRUARY 1

Stapleton, Staten Island becomes a customs-free port.

FEBRUARY 2

The first issue of *Look* magazine, simply dated "February," pictures FDR, Joan Crawford, the miracle of the X-ray, a parolee who "Kills 5—Gets 4 Paroles," and—front and center—a strange picture of Hermann Goering cuddling a lion cub.

FEBRUARY 3

The Good Earth, a film based on Pearl Buck's acclaimed novel of the same name, is named a *New York Times* Critics' Pick, the day after it opened.

FEBRUARY 4

In her column, "My Day," Eleanor Roosevelt writes, "A grand ride this morning, and then luncheon at the National Training School for Girls in the building which WPA work has transformed. I would never have recognized it and the interesting thing is that surroundings seem to have had an effect upon the human beings. The girls looked differently too and there is real teaching going on now which is something to be truly thankful for."

FEBRUARY 5

The first Charlie Chaplin talking picture, *Modern Times,* is released. Chaplin was one of the last holdouts, continuing to make silent films for years after most other auteurs had switched to talkies.

FEBRUARY 6

K. Elizabeth Ohi becomes the first Japanese-American female lawyer.

FEBRUARY 7

Elihu Root, U.S. minister of war and foreign affairs,
and a Nobel Prize winner in 1912, dies at 91.

FEBRUARY 8

The *New York Times* reports that many cases of "delayed-action
blindness" are appearing among soldiers of the Great War,
some 20 years after they were exposed to mustard gas.

FEBRUARY 9

On this day 50 years ago, in Boston, "A case of resurrection of the body was
performed by Superintendent Cornish, of Pinkerton's detective agency . . .
The man who was operated upon is named Henry J. Thomas, and his recall to life
is worth $5,000 to the United States Mutual Accident Association. . . . The body
was found in Cambridge, where it was carefully concealing itself. . . . Inspector
Hauscom Frost felt the hands and face of the late Thomas and then drew back,
whispering 'He's alive.' That settled it, and the company will not pay the policy."

FEBRUARY 10

Ragnhild Hveger, of the Netherlands, sets a world record for
freestyle swimming in the 400 meter (5:14.2). A few days later
she would break the 200-meter record by seven seconds.

FEBRUARY 11

General Motors formally recognizes the United
Automobile Workers Union, ending a sit-down strike.

FEBRUARY 12

The Cleveland (now Los Angeles) Rams are granted an NFL franchise.

FEBRUARY 13

The long-running comic strip *Prince Valiant,* by Hal Foster, debuts.

FEBRUARY 14

Lovers celebrating Valentine's Day probably don't recall
the many unromantic events that share February 14
as an anniversary—the death of Captain James Cook
(1779), President James K. Polk's becoming the first
president to have his photograph taken (1849), and the
admittance of Arizona as a state (1912) being but a few.

FEBRUARY 15

The American Elm becomes the state tree of Nebraska.

FEBRUARY 16

DuPont Corp. patents nylon, developed by employee Wallace H. Carothers.

FEBRUARY 17

The Ice Hockey World Championships begins in London, England. Canada would go on to win the championship title, its ninth.

FEBRUARY 18

Ten workman on the Golden Gate Bridge in San Francisco fall 200 feet to their deaths in the water after a scaffolding collapses.

President Franklin Delano Roosevelt delivers his second inaugural address on the east portico of the U.S. Capitol.

FEBRUARY 19

The Last of Mrs. Cheyney, starring Joan Crawford, is
released to movie theaters. This is a remake of a 1929 film
by the actress Crawford considered her rival, Norma Shearer.

FEBRUARY 20

Future winner of the Nobel Prize in Chemistry
(1988) Robert Huber is born in Munich, Germany.

FEBRUARY 21

The world's first successful flying car, Waldo
Waterman's Aerobile, makes its maiden flight.

FEBRUARY 22

The Cleveland Rams professional football team,
which began playing in 1936, joins the NFL.

FEBRUARY 23

On this day in 1917, U.S. ambassador Walter Page receives the cipher text
and translation of the Zimmerman Telegram—a secret message from Germany
to Mexico, requesting that the countries join together to make war against
the United States. The message was intercepted and decoded by the British.

FEBRUARY 24

The first U.S. group hospital and medical
cooperative is authorized in Washington, D.C.

FEBRUARY 25

The American Friends Service Committee (the Quakers) announce plans to
set up an "idle miner colony" in Pennsylvania. The Quakers estimate that some
200,000 miners are not only currently out of work, but will never again work in
the mines, though that it is all they know how to do. Under their plan, families in
the colony would have enough to subsist on while the fathers learn new trades.

FEBRUARY 26

Christopher Isherwood and W.H. Auden's *Ascent
of F6: A Tragedy in Two Acts* premieres in London

FEBRUARY 27

On this day a year ago, the writer George Orwell was in Wigan, England, a
place of "frightful slag-heaps and belching chimneys," researching the effects
of the Depression on the distressed areas of Northern England. The resulting
book, the controversial *Road to Wigan Pier,* would be published in March 1937.

FEBRUARY 28

Aviator Ted Herbert flies over midtown Manhattan
in a sport plane operated by a V-8 automobile engine.

MARCH 1

The first permanent automobile
license plates are issued in Connecticut.

MARCH 2

Lost Horizon, an ambitious film adaptation of the James Hilton novel,
is released in theaters. Ronald Colman and Jane Wyatt star in this
fantasy about travelers who accidentally stumble upon Shangri-La.

MARCH 3

Bobby Driscoll, who would become famous as a
child actor in many Disney live-action pictures, is born.

MARCH 4

Jazz bassist Ron Carter *(Ron Carter
Meets Bach)* is born in Ferndale, Michigan.

MARCH 5

Lyndon Baines Johnson launches his campaign for state
representative from the Old Main auditorium at his alma
mater, Southwest State Teachers College (now Texas State).

MARCH 6

Valentina V. Tereshkova-Nikolayev, who would
be the first woman in space *(Vostok 6),* is born.

MARCH 7

Scottish actress Anne Kristen *(Coronation
Street, Hamish Macbeth)* is born.

Horror writer H.P. Lovecraft dies on March 15 at age 38. His macabre works go on to influence generations of writers and artists (the "Arkham" sign in this illustration is a reference to a "witch-cursed, legend-haunted" town in Lovecraft's stories).

MARCH 8

Britain's George VI, in the run-up to his coronation as
king of the United Kingdom and the Dominions of the British
Commonwealth on May 12, is featured on the cover of *Time* magazine.

MARCH 9

In western Ohio a 5.4 earthquake takes
place—the most severe in Ohio's history.

MARCH 10

An audience of 21,000 jams the Paramount
Theatre in New York City to see Benny Goodman.
Goodman is crowned "King of Swing" on this night.

MARCH 11

Joseph S. Cullinan, American oil industrialist
and founder of Texaco (b. 1860), dies.

MARCH 12

Baseball player Joe DiMaggio, after being one of the first
rookies in history to hold out for more money, signs with the
Yankees for a reported $17,500, just in time for spring training.

MARCH 13

The cover of the *New Yorker* depicts a man working on his income
taxes. Over one shoulder, the ghosts of Washington, Franklin,
and Lincoln look on; over the other, dreams of cars and vacations
tempt him. The average wage-earner's income is just over $1,000.

MARCH 14

In what is humorously termed the "Battle of the
Century," Fred Allen and Jack Benny meet on the radio.

MARCH 15

H.P. Lovecraft (b. 1890), the Rhode Island author whose works of horror
and the paranormal would shape the future of weird fiction, dies.
Among Lovecraft's legacies are the Cthulhu mythos and the *Necronomicon*.

MARCH 16

Aviatrix Amelia Earhart's 27,000-mile flight around
the globe is postponed due to a storm at sea.

MARCH 17

Sir Austen Chamberlain (b. 1863), English statesman
and recipient of the 1925 Nobel Peace Prize, dies.

MARCH 18

A gas explosion at a school in New
London, Texas, results in 296 fatalities.

MARCH 19

The Canadian House of Commons passes a bill
banning Canadian enlistment in the Spanish Civil War.

MARCH 20

The Franco offensive takes place in Guadalajara, Spain.

MARCH 21

In the "Ponce Massacre," 18 people and a seven-year-old girl
in Ponce, Puerto Rico, are gunned down by a police squad acting
under the orders of U.S.-appointed governor Blanton C. Winship.

MARCH 22

Ten-year-old Jacqueline Jones of Atlanta, the
niece of a newspaper man traveling with President
Roosevelt's party, gets quite a surprise when she
meets the president of the United States and is
allowed to place a flower in the buttonhole of his jacket.

MARCH 23

The Los Angeles Railway Co. starts using
Presidents' Conference Committee (PCC) streetcars.

February brings some of the worst flooding in the history of Arkansas. More than 17,000 refugee families rapidly fill the 75 camps established to shelter them.

MARCH 24

Chick Webb & His Orchestra
record "That Naughty Waltz."

MARCH 25

The *Washington Daily News* becomes the first
U.S. newspaper with a perfumed advertising page.

MARCH 26

William H. Hastie becomes the first African-American federal judge when
FDR appoints him to the United States District Court for the Virgin Islands.

MARCH 27

Future pro wrestler Kenny Benkowski, who would
come to be known as "Sodbuster Kenny Jay" or "The Very
Capable Kenny Jay," is born in Holdingford, Minnesota.

MARCH 28

Three students at the University of Wisconsin have
their first "real" food after many weeks of subsisting
on nothing but raw milk and fruit. The students
were participating in an experiment at the university.

MARCH 29

Lion-tamer-turned-circus-owner and celebrity Clyde Beatty appears on the cover of *Time* magazine holding a lion cub, with the caption "Clyde Beatty and Captive."

MARCH 30

A report to Canada's House of Commons estimates that the population of the northerly country has reached more than 11 million.

MARCH 31

Foreshadowing the brutal destruction of the Spanish town of Guernica, the city of Durango is bombed by German and Italian forces supporting Spanish Nationalist troops. Scores of civilians are killed.

APRIL 1

French astronomer Marguerite Laugier discovers asteroid 1426.

APRIL 2

Today is the 72nd anniversary of the Union victory at Petersburg, Virginia. U.S. Grant's army attacked the Confederates around 7 a.m. Robert E. Lee sent a telegram to Jefferson Davis in Richmond, Virginia, saying, "I think it is absolutely necessary that we should abandon our position tonight." The fall of Petersburg ensured the capture of Richmond the next day. General Lee would surrender April 9.

APRIL 3

Warner Bros. animated character Petunia Pig makes her debut in the eight-minute *Merrie Melodies* episode "Porky's Romance."

APRIL 4

Byron Nelson wins the fourth Golf Masters Championship, shooting a 283.

APRIL 5

An announcement is made to national newspapers that an airplane intended for scientific experiments in the stratosphere is nearly complete. The plane, built by Lockheed, will be delivered to the U.S. Army.

APRIL 6

The counterfeit Francis Drake brass plate is presented at a meeting of the California Historical Society, perpetuating a hoax that had been intended as a joke.

APRIL 7

Jazz and rock singer "Big" Charlie Thomas (The Drifters) is born in New York.

APRIL 8

Seymour Hersh, Pulitzer Prize–winning investigative reporter, is born.

APRIL 9

The *Kamikaze-go* arrives at Croydon Airport in London,
becoming the first Japanese-built aircraft to fly to Europe.

Colin Luther Powell is born on April 25 in Harlem, New York. He will grow up to be
General Colin Powell (pictured here), and will eventually be the 65th U.S. secretary of state.

APRIL 10

American actor, director, and screenwriter
Ralph Ince dies in a car accident in London.

APRIL 11

A explosion at the Charles A. Krause corn mill in Milwaukee,
Wisconsin, sends half of the 60 people who were in the mill at
the time to the hospital. Two are known dead, while 8 to 12 are
unaccounted for and believed to be trapped beneath tons of debris.

APRIL 12

British modernist author Virginia Woolf appears on the cover of
Time magazine, in honor of the publication of her novel *The Years*.

APRIL 13

In the aftermath of the massive flooding in the Ohio River Valley,
Merrill Bernard, chief of the River and Flood Division of the
Weather Bureau, announces that the service will be expanded
to provide modern, up-to-date methods of forecasting floods.

APRIL 14

An address delivered at the World Textile Conference reveals that reducing
the hours of textile workers to 40 per week has not caused the predicted
increases in labor costs or decreases in profits. Meanwhile, the House Labor
Committee votes 11–4 in favor of a resolution condemning sit-down strikers.

APRIL 15

The Detroit Red Wings retain the Stanley Cup,
beating the New York Rangers 3–0 in the
fifth and deciding game of the series.

APRIL 16

A.S. Beck Shoe Stores, following a trend among shoe chains, announce
a price increase of 47 cents, up to $4.45, for a pair of shoes in its stores.

APRIL 17

Cartoon character Daffy Duck makes his screen debut in "Porky's
Duck Hunt," a nine-minute *Merrie Melodies* cartoon by Warner Bros.

APRIL 18

Per yesterday's order by the ASPCA, high-fashion hat-maker Lilly
Daché must dig up the cornerstone of her new building in New
York City and remove the live horned toad from the box she
had interred there as a time capsule. Based on the spurious report
of a horned toad in Texas that had lived 125 years in a similar box,
she believed the toad would survive and would bring her good luck.

APRIL 19

The 41st Boston Marathon is won by Walter
Young of Canada, with a time of 2:33:20.

APRIL 20

In response to Japan's barely concealed efforts at fortifying the southern tip of Formosa, Great Britain elects to pour millions of pounds into the fortification of Hong Kong.

APRIL 21

A study completed at Harvard University finds that the first quarter of the 20th century was the "bloodiest period in all history."

APRIL 22

New York City college students stage their fourth annual peace strike.

APRIL 23

Former president Theodore Roosevelt, speaking at the Sorbonne in Paris, says, "The leaders of thought and of action grope their way forward to a new life, realizing, sometimes dimly, sometimes clear-sightedly, that the life of material gain, whether for a nation or an individual, is of value only as a foundation, only as there is added to it the uplift that comes from devotion to loftier ideals."

APRIL 24

The cover of today's *Saturday Evening Post* features a Norman Rockwell illustration of a ticket agent seemingly dreaming of the destinations he'd like to travel to.

APRIL 25

American air-show daredevil Clem Sohn dies at 26
when his chute fails to open during a stunt in France.

APRIL 26

The Basque town of Guernica is mercilessly bombed by German and Italian
air squadrons in an attack targeting civilians to create terror. Pablo Picasso
would create a masterful anti-war painting memorializing the attack.

On May 6, the German passenger airship LZ 129 *Hindenburg* catches fire and is destroyed; 35
of the 97 people on board, along with a member of the ground crew, are killed.

APRIL 27

The U.S. Social Security system
makes its first benefit payment.

APRIL 28

Pan Am makes the first commercial
flight across the Pacific.

APRIL 29

Actor William Gillette (b. 1853), who
portrayed Sherlock Holmes on stage, dies.

APRIL 30

General Douglas MacArthur marries Jean Faircloth in
a civil ceremony. Jean was the general's second wife.

MAY 1

President Roosevelt signs the Neutrality Act,
which forbids Americans to travel on
belligerent craft, among other restrictions.

MAY 2

John Davison Rockefeller, American industrialist and
philanthropist, dies at 97 in Ormond Beach, Florida.

MAY 3

Identical twins William and Robert Mauch, dressed as their characters
in the upcoming movie version of Mark Twain's novel *The Prince
and the Pauper,* are featured on the cover of *Time* magazine,
in conjunction with the article "Mauch Twins and Mark Twain."

MAY 4

Noel Rosa, Brazilian songwriter (b. 1910), dies.

MAY 5

Many years hence, on November 23, 1963, British science-fiction fans will hear
the theme music to the BBC's *Doctor Who* for the first time. Delia Derbyshire,
who will arrange the music, is born on this day in 1937 in Coventry, England.

MAY 6

The German passenger airship *Hindenburg* catches fire while attempting to
dock at the Lakehurst (New Jersey) Naval Air Station after a three-day trip
from Frankfurt, Germany. It takes only about 30 seconds for the craft to be
completely destroyed. Of the 97 people on board, 35 (13 passengers,
22 crew) are killed, along with one member of the ground crew.

MAY 7

Today marks the 22nd anniversary of the sinking of the British ocean liner *Lusitania* by a German submarine.

MAY 8

War Admiral, under jockey Charles Kurtsinger, wins the Kentucky Derby, en route to winning the Triple Crown.

MAY 9

Edgar Bergen and his dummy sidekick, Charlie McCarthy, began a 19-year run (through July 11, 1956) as part of the *Chase and Sanborn Hour*.

MAY 10

Colonel Matt Winn, president of Churchill Downs race course, is shown on the front cover of *Time* magazine along with four of the favorites in the recently run Kentucky Derby.

MAY 11

Today is the 10th anniversary of the founding of the Academy of Motion Picture Arts and Sciences, which every year distributes the Academy Awards.

MAY 12

Today is the 33rd birthday of Spanish Surrealist painter Salvador Dali, who was born in 1904 in the town of Figueres, Catalonia.

MAY 13

On his 23rd birthday, heavyweight boxer Joe Louis (b. May 13, 1914) is barely a month away from winning the world championship—which he will hold until 1949, the longest run of any heavyweight fighter.

On May 27, a motorcycle brigade leads the way as the first automobiles ceremoniously cross San Francisco's Golden Gate Bridge.

MAY 14

A&P Food Stores announce that, starting tomorrow night, the company will enact a policy of a shorter work week for employees, and most of the Eastern division's stores (more than 2,000) will close at 8 p.m.

MAY 15

War Admiral and jockey Charles Kurtsinger win the Preakness, the second jewel in the Triple Crown.

MAY 16

Future ballet dancer and actress Yvonne Craig is born in Taylorville, Illinois. She will be best known for her role as Batgirl on the 1960s *Batman* TV series.

MAY 17

Some 5,000 Japanese Buddhist worshippers and 40 priests give thanks to the spirits of cotton plants and silkworms for providing such basic needs to humankind through their sacrifices.

MAY 18

In a year rife with labor upheavals, the seamen of the Lykes Brothers shipping line—the largest fleet in the Gulf of Mexico—call a strike, while the governor of Maine withdraws National Guard troops from the shoe-strike area around Lewiston-Auburn.

MAY 19

It is announced that the U.S. president's offices
have been equipped with an electric alarm
system that allows any of the president's secretaries
to call an armed guard at a moment's notice.

MAY 20

Thousands of families in the Western states reside on
farms that, 75 years ago today, were made possible
when President Abraham Lincoln signed the
Homestead Act. The act gave 160 acres of public
land to settlers who paid a filing fee and had
five years of continuous residence on that
land. Some 600,000 claims were filed by 1900.

MAY 21

The research station North Pole-1 is established
approximately 12 miles from the North Pole. It
is the first of the Soviet manned "drifting stations,"
which move with the ice on which they are
established. North Pole-1 will be manned for
nine months and will drift 1,770 miles.

MAY 22

Two Chicago youths, who were arrested for murdering
26-year-old Ada Carey for $10 after she gave them a lift, are
hustled from their jail Onida, South Dakota, and taken to one
in Pierre, to protect them from the mob assembled outside.

MAY 23

Industrialist and philanthropist John D. Rockefeller
dies at his home in Ormond Beach, Florida,
just a couple of months shy of his 98th birthday.

MAY 24

Future pilot Roger Peterson is born today. He will be just
21 years old when an aircraft he is piloting crashes, killing
Peterson and three famous rock and roll musicians: Buddy
Holly, Ritchie Valens, and J.P. Richardson ("The Big Bopper").

MAY 25

In a press conference, President Roosevelt discusses the
possibility of the government's achieving a monopoly on helium.

MAY 26

Actor John Wayne celebrates his 30th birthday. Five of his
172 pictures will be released this year: *California Straight
Ahead!*, *I Cover the War*, *Idol of the Crowds*, *Adventure's
End*, and *Born to the West* (reissued as *Hell Town*).

MAY 27

The week-long opening celebration for
the Golden Gate Bridge commences.

MAY 28

The swashbuckler *The Prince and the Pauper,* based
on the Mark Twain book and starring Errol Flynn
and the Mauch twins, premieres in movie theaters.

The Resettlement Administration, formed in 1935, sought to
relocate families who were hardest hit by the Depression. In
1937 the RA is folded into the Farm Security Administration,
whose aim is to help improve conditions for farm workers.

MAY 29

Today marks the 201st birthday of Founding Father
Patrick Henry, who was born in Studley, Virginia, in 1736.

MAY 30

Voice actor and comedian Mel Blanc celebrates his 29th birthday today.
Only a little more than two months ago, he made his debut as the voices
of Warner Bros.' Porky Pig and Daffy Duck in *Porky's Duck Hunt*. He would
be best remembered for these and other Warner Bros. characters such
as Bugs Bunny, Tweety Bird, Marvin the Martian, and Pepe Le Pew.

MAY 31

Time magazine's cover features the Dionne quintuplets—the first
quintuplets ever known to have survived. They are pictured surrounding
a large cake in celebration of their third birthday (b. May 28, 1934).

JUNE 1

Amelia Earhart and her navigator Fred Noonan depart Miami,
Florida, bound for California by traveling around the world.

JUNE 2

Louis Vierne (b. 1870), French organist and composer, dies at 66.

JUNE 3

Prince Edward, Duke of Windsor, and divorcée Wallis Warfield Simpson marry at the Château de Candé in France's Loire Valley. A Church of England clergyman conducts the service, which is witnessed by only about 16 guests. Wallis is now the duchess of Windsor, but King George, under pressure from his ministers, denies her the title of "royal highness" enjoyed by her husband.

JUNE 4

Sylvan N. Goldman, owner of the Humpty Dumpty supermarket chain in Oklahoma City, places an ad in the newspapers for his invention, the shopping cart: "It's new. It's sensational. No more baskets to carry."

JUNE 5

War Admiral, a son of Man o' War, wins the Belmont with jockey Charles Kurtsinger, completing his sweep of all three races in the 1937 Triple Crown.

JUNE 6

On this date, four Russians are left on an ice floe 35 miles from the North Pole. They would spend the next 274 days free-floating while conducting scientific experiments.

JUNE 7

Hollywood is shocked to learn of the sudden and tragic death of the actress Jean Harlow, who has succumbed to uremic poisoning (now better known as acute renal failure, or acute kidney failure) at the age of 26.

JUNE 8

A total solar eclipse occurs.

JUNE 9

The Oscar Hammerstein II–Jerome Kern collaboration "Allegheny Al," written for the Western movie *High, Wide and Handsome,* receives official copyright protection today.

JUNE 10

Robert Laird Borden, eighth prime minister of Canada (b. 1854), dies.

JUNE 11

The Marx brothers' comedy classic *A Day at the Races* is released. In 2000, the American Film Institute would rank this movie as number 59 among the funniest movies of all time.

JUNE 12

Following a full year of broadcasting the new-fangled "swing" music to radio listeners, Columbia Broadcasting Systems holds an anniversary concert featuring performances by, among others, Benny Goodman, Duke Ellington, and Bunny Berigan. The Quintet of the Hot Club of France, featuring Stéphane Grappelli and Django Reinhardt, is broadcast via shortwave radio from France.

JUNE 13

Joe DiMaggio hits three consecutive home runs against the St. Louis Browns.

JUNE 14

Flag Day is not an official federal holiday, though today
Pennsylvania becomes the first (and only) U.S. state to celebrate
Flag Day as a state holiday, beginning in the town of Rennerdale.

On May 30, police response to an industrial strike in Chicago turns violent.
Ten civilians are killed and dozens are injured. The incident would later be
called the Memorial Day Massacre.

JUNE 15

Country music legend Waylon Jennings
is born on this day in Littlefield, Texas.

JUNE 16

The Cradle Will Rock, a musical allegory about corruption
written by Mark Blitzstein under the auspices of the Federal
Theater Project and directed by Orson Welles, is scheduled
to open this night, but is prevented from doing so due to
political pressure. It runs the next night at a non-FTP theater.

JUNE 17

Movie musical star Jeanette MacDonald marries singer and actor Gene
Raymond in one of the best-attended Hollywood weddings of the decade.

JUNE 18

Gaston Doumergue, premier/president of France (1913–1934),
dies. He was the first president of France to marry while in office.

JUNE 19

James M. Barrie, Scottish novelist and dramatist,
and creator of the beloved *Peter Pan,* dies.

JUNE 20

Enigmatic blues musician Robert Johnson, considered
to be one of the most influential bluesmen of all time,
makes his final recordings: 17 takes of 10 different tunes.

JUNE 21

The Wimbledon Championships are
televised for the first time, by the BBC.

JUNE 22

Joe Louis wins his first heavyweight
championship, against James J. Braddock.

JUNE 23

Future Nobel Peace Prize (2008) winner
Martti Ahtisaari is born in Viipuri, Finland.

JUNE 24

Liechtenstein, a land-locked principality located totally
within the Alps, officially adopts its national flag.

JUNE 25

English actor Colin Clive (b. 1900), famous as Dr. Frankenstein
in the classic films *Frankenstein* (1931) and *Bride of
Frankenstein* (1935), dies at 39 of complications from tuberculosis.

JUNE 26

John J. "Black Jack" Pershing (U.S. general in World War I;
Republican candidate for president, 1920) celebrates the
32nd anniversary of his marriage to Helen Frances Warren.

JUNE 27

This week the Warner Bros. film *Another Dawn*, starring Errol Flynn and Kay
Francis, premieres. In previous Warner Bros. movies, whenever a movie marquee
was shown on screen, it always featured a fictitious film called *Another Dawn*.
The studio finally decided to make a real movie to match the made-up title.

JUNE 28

Time magazine's cover for the week features Ethel du Pont
and Franklin Roosevelt Jr., in conjunction with the story
of their wedding, dubbed "Wedding-of-the-Year" by *Time*.

JUNE 29

Canadian prime minister W.L. Mackenzie King meets with Hermann
Göring and, later in the day, Adolf Hitler; in his diary he would
call June 29, 1937, "perhaps the most significant day in my life."

JUNE 30

The Emergency 999 telephone service is started in the United Kingdom.

JULY 1

President Roosevelt, wife Eleanor, and their family have lunch with Mr. and Mrs. Eugene du Pont Jr., the parents of their soon-to-be daughter-in-law.

Screen siren Jean Harlow, visiting the Capitol on January 29, playfully grabs Senator Robert Reynolds for a "love scene." Just a few months later the actress would die of kidney failure at the age of 26.

JULY 2

Pilot Amelia Earhart, the first female to fly the Atlantic, and her navigator, Fred L. Noonan, disappear over the Pacific Ocean.

JULY 3

Freling Foster, in *Collier's Weekly*, notes that, while "in the early days of this country" nearly all American families owned their houses or farms, "today about three quarters of all city dwellers rent their homes and about half of the farmers lease their lands."

JULY 4

Universal's *I Cover the War*, starring John Wayne, Gwen Gaze, and Don Barclay, is released.

JULY 5

SPAM (formerly—and unsuccessfully—named "Spiced Ham") is introduced by George A. Hormel & Co. Seventy years later, the 7 billionth can of SPAM would be sold.

JULY 6

The July 6 issue of *Look* Magazine features "America's Most Modern Girl's College" (Sarah Lawrence College), Bing Crosby's "true story told in rare pictures," a photo comparison of "how television has improved" (1929, 1931, 1934, and 1937), and other entertaining fare.

JULY 7

In the "Marco Polo Bridge Incident," a battle between the Chinese and Japanese armies erupts into a conflict that would last nearly 10 years.

JULY 8

Mary Dell, writing in Britain's *Daily Mirror*, comments on one of the most popular authors of the day, Agatha Christie, and her new Hercule Poirot novel, *Dumb Witness* (marketed in the United States as *Poirot Loses a Client*): "This is Agatha Christie at her best. . . . Here's a book that will keep all thriller fans happy from page one to page three hundred and something."

JULY 9

Oliver Law (b. 1899), American labor organizer and the first African-American commander of U.S. troops, is killed in the Spanish Civil War.

JULY 10

The International Exposition in Paris features a demonstration of high-definition television (455 lines).

JULY 11

Distinguished pianist and composer George Gershwin dies at 38. Gershwin is remembered for works such as *Rhapsody in Blue, An American in Paris,* and *Porgy and Bess.*

JULY 12

The July 12, 1937, cover of the newsweekly *Time* magazine features a portrait of James E. West, the first professional Chief Scout Executive of the Boy Scouts of America.

JULY 13

The first Krispy Kreme doughnut store opens for business in Winston-Salem, North Carolina.

JULY 14

"On the morning of July 14, 1937, a maid entered the Methodist Building, across the street from the Capitol. When she turned the key to the apartment of her client, the Senate majority leader, a terrible sight awaited her. There sprawled on the floor . . . was the pajama-clad body of Arkansas Senator Joseph Taylor Robinson . . . succumbed to heart disease." (U.S. Senate, *Art & History*)

JULY 15

The first 149 inmates arrive at the German Ettersberg prison, soon to be renamed Buchenwald Concentration Camp.

JULY 16

The silver screen comedy *Topper* is released. Based on the saucy novel by Thorne Smith, the movie stars Constance Bennett and Cary Grant as free-spirited ghosts who shake up the staid life of banker Cosmo Topper (Roland Young). Two movie sequels and a TV series would eventually follow.

JULY 17

Illustrating America's fascination with European sociopolitics, among the book reviews in the *Saturday Review of Literature,* July 17, 1937, are one on *The Spirit and Structure of German Fascism* and one on *The Magic of Monarchy.*

On June 19 James M. Barrie, author of *Peter Pan and Wendy,* dies in London. His story of a boy who wouldn't grow up has already appeared in myriad forms, including the 1924 silent film advertised by this poster.

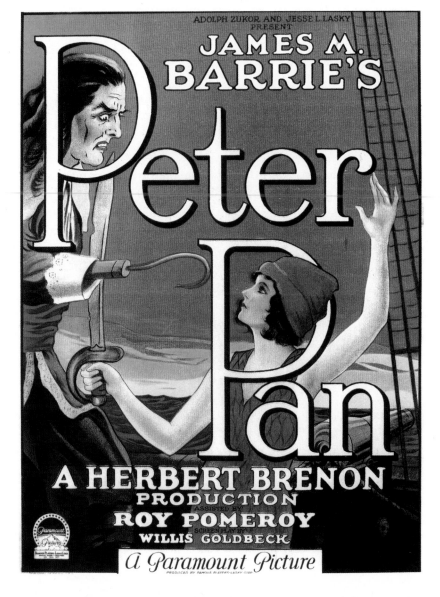

JULY 18

Future winner of the 1981 Nobel Prize in Chemistry
Roald Hoffmann is born in Zloczov, Poland.

JULY 19

Union leader Harry Bridges is featured
on the cover of *Time* magazine.

JULY 20

Guglielmo Marconi (b. 1874), Italian-born inventor of the
radio and recipient of the 1909 Nobel Prize in Physics,
dies after a series of heart attacks. In tribute, radio
stations around the world observe two minutes of silence.

JULY 21

First Lady Eleanor Roosevelt spends the afternoon in New
Lebanon, New York, admiring arts and crafts at a local exhibition.

JULY 22

The U.S. Senate votes down the Judicial Procedures Reform
Bill of 1937, by which President Roosevelt would have added
six more (politically appointed) justices to the Supreme Court.

JULY 23

Saratoga, Jean Harlow's last film, is released. Also starring Clark Gable, the movie was completed with a double standing in for Harlow in the scenes shot after the young star's tragic death.

JULY 24

In theaters this week is the romantic comedy *The Lady Escapes,* starring George Sanders and Gloria Stuart. Decades later, Stuart's career would be revived with her appearance in James Cameron's *Titanic.*

JULY 25

A congressional committee favorably recommends enacting Senate Bill 2067 and the House companion bill, HR. 7931. The law would be passed August 5, creating the National Cancer Institute.

JULY 26

Future winner of the 1996 Nobel Prize in Physics Robert C. Richardson is born in Washington, D.C.

JULY 27

Think Fast, Mr. Moto, the first of a series of eight mystery movies about the Japanese sleuth, premieres in theaters. The title role is played by unmistakable character actor Peter Lorre, whose heritage is Jewish and Austrian, not Asian. The second Mr. Moto film would be released on December 24 of this year.

JULY 28

Japanese forces succeed in taking control of
Beijing (Peking), defeating Chinese Nationalist forces.

JULY 29

Future winner of the Sveriges Riksbank Prize in Economic Sciences in
Memory of Alfred Nobel (2000) Daniel L. McFadden is born in Raleigh, N.C.

JULY 30

Wee Willie Winkie is released in movie theaters. It stars Shirley Temple, the
country's top box-office draw of the year, according to *Motion Picture Herald*.

JULY 31

Norman Rockwell's illustration for the cover of the *Saturday Evening
Post* with today's date is called "At the Auction" or "Found Treasure."

AUGUST 1

In an early consolidation of the airline industry, National Parks
Airways is taken over by Western Air Express, later Western Air Lines.
WAE, itself a spinoff of TWA after an earlier merger of Transcontinental
Air Transport and Western Air Express, would survive as Western
Airlines until the late 1980s, when it would be taken over by Delta.

AUGUST 2

The Marihuana Tax Act of 1937 (Pub. 238, 7th Cong., 50 Stat. 551), which places a tax on the sale of cannabis, is passed.

AUGUST 3

Former U.S. senator Roland Burris, appointed to fill the Senate seat vacated when Barack Obama was elected president of the United States in 2008 by the disgraced governor of Illinois Rod Blagojevich, is born this day in 1937.

On July 2, Amelia Earhart and navigator Fred Noonan disappear during Earhart's attempt to become the first woman to fly around the world. Their bodies are never found.

AUGUST 4

The Marine Corps League, founded in 1923, today
receives a federal charter as a veteran's organization.

AUGUST 5

Herb Brooks, who coached the 1980 Men's Olympic hockey
team to an epic upset of the U.S.S.R., skates into the world today.

AUGUST 6

Stella Dallas, one of the all-time great tearjerkers,
premieres in movie theaters—a triumph for
star Barbara Stanwyck, who would receive an
Academy Award nomination for her performance.

AUGUST 7

Du Barry Did All Right, a 22-minute comedy by
Warner Bros. starring Irene Bordoni, is released.

AUGUST 8

The Bonneville Dam on the Columbia
River begins producing power.

AUGUST 9

A memorial concert to George Gershwin, who died on
July 11, is held in New York, featuring luminaries such as
Otto Klemperer, Al Jolson, Fred Astaire, and José Iturbi.

AUGUST 10

The first patent for an electric guitar is granted
to G.D. Beauchamp of the Electro String Corporation.

AUGUST 11

The Life of Emile Zola is released in American movie
theaters. Starring Paul Muni, it would be only the
second biographical film to win a Best Picture Oscar.

AUGUST 12

An African-American writer of young adult literature,
the oft-awarded Walter Dean Myers is born.

AUGUST 13

Up to this point a series of small but dangerous skirmishes,
the second Sino-Japanese War begins in earnest with the
engagement of Japanese and Chinese troops at Shanghai.

AUGUST 14

The Appalachian Trail becomes a single continuous entity with the completion of the last segment in Sugarloaf Mountain, Maine.

AUGUST 15

The *Air Commerce Bulletin* publishes the Commerce Department's report on the *Hindenburg* disaster, concluding that "the cause of the accident was the ignition of a mixture of free hydrogen and air," probably caused by a leak.

AUGUST 16

A veritable who's-who of early Hollywood luminaries work on a film adaptation of *Romeo and Juliet,* including George Cukor, Norma Shearer, Leslie Howard, and John Barrymore; the film opens nationwide one year after its limited preview.

AUGUST 17

Hugo Black receives confirmation by the U.S. Senate after his appointment by President Roosevelt as an associate justice of the United States Supreme Court.

AUGUST 18

The United States issues a first-class rate postage stamp to honor the 350th anniversary of the founding of Roanoke colony and the birth of Virginia Dare, the first documented child born in the New World to English parents.

AUGUST 19

The Auxiliary to the National Medical Association (ANMA), originally organized in Philadelphia, Pennsylvania, in 1936, elects Alma Wells Givens its first president and proclaims her to be a founder of the organization (which is still active today).

AUGUST 20

President Roosevelt signs the Bonneville Power Act, ensuring that energy derived from publicly funded hydroelectric projects would be sold to the public, over the objections of private corporations in the energy industry.

Beginning July 2 at midnight, the first of what will be continuous 24-hour guards is posted at the Tomb of the Unknowns. The guard protects the dignity of the site, but does not prevent visitors, like this sailor and his girl, from paying their respects.

AUGUST 21

Award-winning novelist Robert Stone *(Dog Soldiers)*, called by some one of America's greatest living writers, is born on this day.

AUGUST 22

Malachi Favors, bass player for free-jazz pioneers Art Ensemble of Chicago, is born.

AUGUST 23

Recent college graduates Bill Hewlett and David Packard meet to discuss ideas for a new business. While the actual product to sell and produce is not decided, the core business principles that would underlie Hewlett-Packard Company are laid out for the first time.

AUGUST 24

Supernova 1937C is discovered on this date, having arisen from the star IC 4182; it provides valuable baseline data on type 1a supernovae for years to come.

AUGUST 25

The Brotherhood of Sleeping Car Porters signs its first collective bargaining agreement with Pullman.

AUGUST 26

Andrew W. Mellon (b. 1855), American banker
and U.S. Secretary of the Treasury, dies.

AUGUST 27

The crime drama *Dead End* premieres. Starring Humphrey
Bogart and Joel McCrea, this gritty film is the debut of the
youngsters who would become known as the Dead End Kids.

AUGUST 28

Confession, a "women's picture" starring Kay Francis and Basil Rathbone,
is released. Two years later, Rathbone would make his first appearance on
the big screen as Sherlock Holmes, the role most associated with him.

AUGUST 29

Twentieth Century Fox releases *Thin Ice,* starring
Norwegian ice skater Sonja Henie in her second
major role, alongside leading man Tyrone Power.

AUGUST 30

Future Formula 1 race car driver, designer,
engineer, and inventor Bruce McClaren is born.

AUGUST 31

Mopar, the "parts-and-services" subgroup of Chrysler Group, is established as a separate brand, still in existence today.

SEPTEMBER 1

The Housing Act of 1937, sometimes called the Wagner-Steagall Act, provides for subsidies to be paid from the U.S. government to local public housing agencies (LHAs) to improve living conditions for low-income families.

SEPTEMBER 2

Pierre de Frédy, Baron de Coubertin (b. 1863), widely hailed as the father of the modern Olympic Games, dies at 74. Coubertin founded the International Olympic Committee in 1894 and served as its second president.

SEPTEMBER 3

The seagoing drama *Souls at Sea* premieres. Starring Gary Cooper and George Raft, the film would be nominated for three Academy Awards.

SEPTEMBER 4

Appearing in movie theaters this week is the latest film to feature the popular character Bulldog Drummond, *Bulldog Drummond Comes Back,* with screen legend John Barrymore in a supporting role and John Howard in his first appearance as Drummond.

SEPTEMBER 5

The musical comedy film *One Hundred Men and a Girl* is released.
The girl of the title is popular young singing star Deanna Durbin.

SEPTEMBER 6

Generalissimo Francisco Franco is featured on the cover
of *Time* magazine, in conjunction with the article "El Caudillo."

A sign outside a store in Belle Glade, Florida, reads "100 been pickers wanted." During the
heart of the Depression, seasonal and migrant work is often the only work to be had.

SEPTEMBER 7

Adolf Hitler declares the Treaty of Versailles, which in 1919 had brought hostilities between Germany and the Allies to a close, invalid.

SEPTEMBER 8

Archie Goodwin, a legendary writer and editor in the comic book industry especially known for his work with *Star Wars* material, graphic novels, and the *Manhunter* title, is born.

SEPTEMBER 9

National Football League Hall of Fame defensive back and football coach Dick LeBeau, one of the greatest defensive coordinators the game has seen, enters the world.

SEPTEMBER 10

New gates are installed at the White House to prevent tipsy motorists from crashing through them—evidently a persistent problem.

SEPTEMBER 11

Despite not knowing about the National Football League draft, "Slingin'" Sammy Baugh agrees to join the Washington Redskins as a professional football player on this day, signing a contract right out of college that makes him the highest-paid player on the team. He would go on to revolutionize football, helping make the forward pass a staple of the modern game.

SEPTEMBER 12

The wine appellation Beaujolais is officially recognized in France.

SEPTEMBER 13

The world welcomes Fred Silverman, a member of the Academy of Television Arts and Sciences Hall of Fame for his work as an executive at all three major networks, including greenlighting shows such as *All in the Family, Good Times, Charlie's Angels,* the *Roots* miniseries, *Hill Street Blues,* and *Diff'rent Strokes.*

SEPTEMBER 14

First Lady Eleanor Roosevelt's "My Day" column laments, "No one talks of anything these days except the very precarious situation in which the entire world seems to be floundering."

SEPTEMBER 15

Robert E. Lucas Jr., future winner of the Sveriges Riksbank Prize in Economic Sciences in Memory of Alfred Nobel (1995), is born in Yakima, Washington.

SEPTEMBER 16

Having moved south from Boston, the Washington Redskins make their professional football debut in Washington, D.C., opening their season with a 13–3 win over the New York Giants.

SEPTEMBER 17

The 175th anniversary of the Battle of Antietam is marked
by a commemorative silver half dollar struck by the U.S. Mint.

SEPTEMBER 18

That Certain Woman premieres. This Prohibition-era
drama stars Bette Davis and Henry Fonda.

SEPTEMBER 19

Earl "Dutch" Clark successfully dropkicks a field goal, the last
time this is believed to have happened in the NFL. He leads
the Detroit Lions to a 16–7 victory over the Chicago Cardinals.

SEPTEMBER 20

Pioneer-era baseball star Harry Stovey passes away. He was
the first player to hit 100 home runs and was equally prolific at
stealing bases, being one of the first players to employ a feet-first slide.

SEPTEMBER 21

The world is introduced to Middle Earth on this
day, as J.R.R. Tolkien's novel *The Hobbit* is published.

SEPTEMBER 22

Ruth Roland, silent-film actress (b. 1892), dies.

World-renowned composer and pianist George Gershwin dies in Los Angeles on July 11 after surgery to remove a brain tumor. He is 38 years old.

SEPTEMBER 23

A stunning boxing showcase occurs today, as promoter Michael Strauss
Jacobs stages the Carnival of Champions at New York's Polo Grounds.
Four world championship bouts are scheduled for the same evening.

SEPTEMBER 24

Dangerously prepared and untested, a drug called Elixir of Sulfanilamide
causes its first American death (of more than 100) on this day. Reactions to
the poisonings lead to the passing of the 1938 Food, Drug, and Cosmetic Act.

SEPTEMBER 25

Destined to become Chief of Staff of the United States Army and a member of
the Joint Chiefs of Staff, General Gordon R. Sullivan is born on this day in Boston.

SEPTEMBER 26

Bessie Smith, the popular and influential African-American
singer known as the "Empress of the Blues" (b. 1894),
dies at 43 years old of injuries sustained in a car crash.

SEPTEMBER 27

On this day, the last known female Balinese tiger is killed, marking
the first extinction of a tiger subspecies in modern times.

SEPTEMBER 28

U.S. patent number 2,094,268 is issued to Joseph B. Friedman for a new invention called the Drinking Tube—the flexible drinking straw.

SEPTEMBER 29

Ray Ewry, American athlete and Olympic medalist, dies at 63.

SEPTEMBER 30

Idol of the Crowds premieres in movie theaters. The film, by Universal Pictures, stars John Wayne, Sheila Bromley, and Charles Brokaw.

OCTOBER 1

The Marihuana Tax Act of 1937, passed on August 2, goes into effect.

OCTOBER 2

Ronald Reagan makes his movie debut in *Love Is on the Air*.

OCTOBER 3

Today Vincent "Randy" Chin is born; before his passing
in 2003, he would help introduce the world to reggae music
through his roles as mentor, producer, and record label founder.

OCTOBER 4

A musician's musician who averaged more than 400 recording sessions a year
from 1965 to 1980, steel guitar master Lloyd Green enters the world on this day.

OCTOBER 5

In a step toward ending American isolationism, President
Roosevelt gives his "Quarantine Speech" in Chicago,
advocating an international "quarantine of aggressor nations."

OCTOBER 6

Future winner of the Nobel Prize in Physiology or
Medicine (2007) Mario R. Capecchi is born in Verona, Italy.

OCTOBER 7

Chet Powers (also known as Dino Valenti and Jesse Oris Farrow),
is born. Powers would write the 1960s anthem "Get Together,"
popularized by the Youngbloods and covered by many others, and
would perform in the psychedelic rock band Quicksilver Messenger Service.

OCTOBER 8

Katharine Hepburn and Ginger Rogers star in the new movie
Stage Door, a comedy-drama about a group of hopeful actresses
living together in a theatrical boarding house. Future stars in
the ensemble include Lucille Ball, Ann Miller, and Eve Arden.

Amateur photography is a relatively affordable pastime, and camera models abound.
This 1937 Certo "Super Sport Dolly" gives the user a choice of two picture sizes, thanks
to interchangeable metal frames or masks.

OCTOBER 9

Ups and Downs, a 21-minute Broadway
Brevities musical, is released by Warner Bros.

OCTOBER 10

New to movie theaters this week is the drama *Lancer Spy*,
which stars George Sanders, Dolores del Rio, and Peter
Lorre. The poster warns, "His Kisses Were Death Traps!"

OCTOBER 11

Businessman, politician, art collector, and horse
breeder Ogden L. Mills passes away, having lived to
see his stables rear the inspirational horse Seabiscuit.

OCTOBER 12

One of golden-age radio's longest-running programs,
Mr. Keen, Tracer of Lost Persons, makes its debut on the
NBC Blue network. It would run through April 1955.

OCTOBER 13

Legendary radio DJ Bruce Morrow, better known as Cousin Brucie, is born.
Morrow would introduce the Beatles at their first Shea Stadium concerts.

OCTOBER 14

Film director Carroll Ballard is born. He would helm quality pictures like *The Black Stallion* (1979) and *Never Cry Wolf* (1983).

OCTOBER 15

The Shirley Temple movie *Heidi,* based on the classic novel by Johanna Spyri, premieres.

OCTOBER 16

Jean de Brunhoff (b. 1899), the French writer and illustrator who created the beloved children's books about the elephant Babar, dies at the age of 37 of tuberculosis.

OCTOBER 17

New to movie theaters this week is the romantic comedy *Double Wedding,* starring frequent costars William Powell and Myrna Loy. This successful screen duo would ultimately appear in 14 films, including the popular *Thin Man* series.

OCTOBER 18

Ernest Hemingway, depicted in a painting as a fisherman, is featured on the cover of *Time* magazine (along with his middle name, Miller).

OCTOBER 19

Illustrator and graphic artist Peter Max
(b. Peter Max Finkelstein) is born in Germany.

OCTOBER 20

Major League Baseball pitcher Juan Marichal (b. Juan
Antonio Marichal Sánchez) is born in the Dominican Republic.
In 1983 he would be inducted into the Baseball Hall of Fame.

OCTOBER 21

Cary Grant and Irene Dunne's sparkling comedy *The Awful Truth* is released.
Its director, Leo McCarey, would win an Academy Award for helming it.

OCTOBER 22

Conquest, a historical drama starring French heartthrob
Charles Boyer as Napoleon Bonaparte, premieres. Also
starring the already legendary Greta Garbo, the film is a success,
but was so expensive to produce that it lost almost $1.4 million.

OCTOBER 23

Premiering in movie theaters this week is *Breakfast for Two,* a
screwball comedy starring Herbert Marshall and Barbara Stanwyck.

OCTOBER 24

Songwriter Cole Porter's life is changed on this day as his legs are crushed in a horseback riding accident, leaving him crippled and in pain for the remainder of his life.

Bessie Smith, known as "the Empress of the Blues," dies on September 26 following a car accident in Clarksdale, Mississippi.

OCTOBER 25

Duke University's football coach Wallace Wade
is featured on the cover of *Time* magazine.

OCTOBER 26

Legendary musicologist Alan Lomax records
fiddler William Stepp's up-tempo version of
"Bonaparte's Retreat." A transcribed version would
be the source of Aaron Copland's famous
"Hoe-Down," from his 1942 ballet *Rodeo*.

OCTOBER 27

Ray Abruzzese is born. His contributions to
the modern popularity of professional football
are still underappreciated today; in fact, the AFL's
New York Jets only signed Abruzzese so that his
college roommate, Joe Namath, would also join the Jets.

OCTOBER 28

Lenny Wilkens is born today in Brooklyn,
New York. He would be elected to the
Naismith Memorial Basketball Hall of Fame three
times: as a player, as a coach, and as assistant
coach for the 1992 Olympic "Dream Team."

OCTOBER 29

Angel, a romantic comedy starring Marlene Dietrich, is released to theaters. Its reception is so lukewarm that star Dietrich would not make another film for two years.

OCTOBER 30

Sir Barton, the first winner of America's horseracing Triple Crown, passes away.

OCTOBER 31

Singer and songwriter Tom Paxton is born. In 2009, he would receive a Lifetime Achievement Award at the 51st Annual Grammy Awards.

NOVEMBER 1

Physicist Ernest Orlando Lawrence (d. 1958), inventor of the atom smasher called the cyclotron, is featured on the cover of *Time* magazine.

NOVEMBER 2

The first official Piper J-2 Club plane is completed on this day, beginning the popular line of Piper Cub designs.

NOVEMBER 3

National Hockey League players stage the
Howie Morenz Memorial Game to raise funds
for the family of Montreal Canadiens star Howie
Morenz, who died after breaking his leg in a game.

NOVEMBER 4

In her "My Day" column, First Lady Eleanor Roosevelt
describes the thrill of receiving a copy of her autobiography
from her publisher. "It looks much more important
than I had ever imagined it would be," she reflects.

NOVEMBER 5

Adolf Hitler holds a conference among his top military leaders
where he clearly states his expansionist, militaristic goals, as
summarized in the Hossbach Memorandum of November 10.

NOVEMBER 6

As the lines are drawn for World War II, Italy, which has already
signed a treaty of peace with Germany, joins Germany and Japan in
union against the Soviet Union when it joins the Anti-Comintern Pact.

NOVEMBER 7

Actor Jean Hersholt's radio drama "Dr. Christian" debuts on CBS's *Vaseline Program,* later renamed *Dr. Christian's Office.* Hersholt created the character himself, naming him after popular author Hans Christian Andersen.

The Life of Emile Zola, starring Paul Muni, opens October 2, en route to becoming the 10th-highest-grossing film of 1937. This cinema, the Carthay Circle Theatre, is also scheduled to host the premier of *Snow White and the Seven Dwarfs* in December.

NOVEMBER 8

James Ramsay MacDonald (b. 1866), British prime minister (Labor Party; 1924, 1929–1935), dies at age 71.

NOVEMBER 9

The Hurricane, starring screen beauty Dorothy Lamour, premieres. Set in the tropics, this is one of the films that cemented Lamour's image as "the sarong girl."

NOVEMBER 10

Following a coup d'état that brought him into power, President Getulio Vargas of Brazil stages a second coup d'état on this date, avoiding scheduled elections.

NOVEMBER 11

Tyrone Power's fourth movie of 1937 opens today, as *Second Honeymoon* hits the screens.

NOVEMBER 12

The United States recognizes its territorial possession of Alaska with the issuance of a three-cent stamp.

NOVEMBER 13

The NBC Symphony Orchestra, a radio
orchestra conducted by maestro Arturo
Toscanini, has its first broadcast this day,
beginning a 17-year run on the airwaves.

NOVEMBER 14

A member of the National Museum of
Dance C.V. Whitney Hall of Fame, Anna
Sokolow appears today in the Broadway
premiere of her "radical dance" performance.

NOVEMBER 15

The American tradition of Sadie Hawkins Day,
when women take the initiative in getting a
date (typically for a Sadie Hawkins Dance), is
introduced by Al Capp in his *Li'l Abner* comic strip.

NOVEMBER 16

Germany tightens restrictions on the
Jewish population; as of this day, German
Jews can receive passports for travel
outside the country only in special cases.

NOVEMBER 17

British comedian Peter Cook is born (d. 1995). Although well known in England for his satiric and anti-establishment humor, which was sometimes controversial, he remains best known to American audiences as the Impressive Clergyman (with speech impediment) in *The Princess Bride* (1987).

NOVEMBER 18

The French royalist terrorist group known as the Cagoulards ("hooded ones") is thwarted in its plot to overthrow the French republic when the government discovers secret plans, caches of weapons, and other incriminating evidence.

NOVEMBER 19

Fred Astaire steps out in *A Damsel in Distress,* a musical comedy that, strangely, features a starlet (Joan Fontaine) who neither sings nor dances.

NOVEMBER 20

Bette Davis has a rare comedic role in the screwball comedy *It's Love I'm After,* in which she and Lesley Howard star as brawling, egotistical actors in love.

NOVEMBER 21

Ingrid Pitt (b. Ingoushka Petrov) is born in Warsaw, Poland. The actress would gain fame in horror movies of the 1960s and 1970s.

NOVEMBER 22

The Vivien Leigh romantic comedy *Storm in a Teacup* opens in U.S. theaters, already having run in England for more than five months. In just over a year (January 1939), Leigh would be announced as the actress chosen to play Scarlett O'Hara.

NOVEMBER 23

Look magazine's cover features Joan Crawford, "Hollywood's Most Interesting Face." Stories inside this issue focus on the Red Cross and eligible bachelors (including Howard Hughes).

On December 12, Japanese bombers sink the USS *Panay*, an American gunboat anchored in the Yangtze River outside Nanking, China.

NOVEMBER 24

In an attempt to end the Second Sino-
Japanese War, the Nine Powers Treaty
Conference (or Brussels Conference) convenes
for the last time, producing a treaty (signed
November 15) and a declaration (dated
November 24), but no practical results.

NOVEMBER 25

Nothing Sacred, destined to be one of the classics of
screwball comedy, premieres. It stars Carole Lombard
as a young woman who becomes the center of a
media circus because of her supposed terminal illness.

NOVEMBER 26

Doctor, astronaut, and hero of the Soviet Union, Boris
Yegorov, the first physician to travel in space, is born on this day.

NOVEMBER 27

In a speech given at the Technical University
of Berlin, Adolf Hitler notes this day as the
start of a period of architectural renewal in
Berlin and describes his plan to "bestow upon
Berlin the streets, edifices, and public areas
it needs to allow it to be fitting and worthy of
being the capital city of the German Reich."

NOVEMBER 28

Noted as one of the best pianists of the late 19th and early 20th centuries, Josef Hofmann gives a Golden Jubilee concert at New York's Metropolitan Opera House, celebrating the 50th anniversary of his New York debut.

NOVEMBER 29

A Warner Bros. character called "Egghead" appears in a seven-minute *Merrie Melodies* episode, "Egghead Rides Again." According to many, Egghead would evolve into the highly popular character Elmer J. Fudd.

NOVEMBER 30

English film director Sir Ridley Scott, the man behind *Alien* and *Blade Runner,* among other hit movies, is born on this day in 1937.

DECEMBER 1

Actor Charleston Lewis ("Chuck") Low is born in New York City. The character actor's most notable role would be Morrie Kessler in *Goodfellas.*

DECEMBER 2

Fans of Laurel and Hardy may remember that today is the 10th anniversary of their first film, *Putting Pants on Philip.* The 19-minute comedy follows J. Piedmont Mumblethunder (Hardy), who must persuade his nephew from Scotland (Laurel) to trade his kilt for pants.

DECEMBER 3

Austrian/English psychoanalyst
Anna Freud turns 40 today.

DECEMBER 4

The British children's comic *The Dandy* is first published. By the 2000s, it would become the world's third longest-running comic.

DECEMBER 5

Tipplers have reason to raise a cup today, which
marks the fourth anniversary of the repeal of Prohibition.

DECEMBER 6

Today is the 60th anniversary of the day on
which Thomas Edison made one of the earliest recordings
of a human voice (reciting "Mary Had a Little Lamb").

DECEMBER 7

In a press conference today, Treasury secretary Henry Morgenthau
tries to ease concerns over data the Bureau of Internal
Revenue is gathering on large income class assets. Morgenthau
pledges that the data collection is not related to a planned tax
on capital assets and that it will not be publicized in any way.

DECEMBER 8

Some 300 Chinese soldiers are trapped by Japanese troops on a peak
12 miles from Nanking. Nearly all the Chinese soldiers are killed in the fight.

Out-of-work artists are employed by the Works Progress Administration
to create public art, including murals, paintings, and posters (like the one
pictured, calling for workplace safety).

FAILURE HERE MAY
MEAN DEATH BELOW
SAFETY FIRST

WPA
FEDERAL ART PROJECT
PENNSYLVANIA

DECEMBER 9

The Japanese military drops leaflets onto
the walled city of Nanking urging the city to
surrender within 24 hours or face annihilation.

DECEMBER 10

A boy named Bobby Dan Blocker in O'Donnell, Texas, is nine
years old today. He would grow up to get a master's degree
in the dramatic arts and land the role for which he would be
best remembered, Eric "Hoss" Cartwright, in the TV series *Bonanza*.

DECEMBER 11

Italy withdraws from the League of Nations.

DECEMBER 12

Japanese naval aircraft attack and sink the USS *Panay*, an American
Navy gunboat anchored in the Yangtze River outside Nanking.

DECEMBER 13

The Nanking Massacre takes place. Japanese troops
begin carrying out several weeks of mass murder
and rape of Chinese civilians in the city of Nanking.

DECEMBER 14

Today is Alabama Day, a state holiday commemorating
Alabama's admittance to the Union in 1819.

DECEMBER 15

Newspapers report that the effective silence from Nanking is
deeply disturbing, and Chinese and U.S. military leaders fear the worst.

DECEMBER 16

Theodore Cole and Ralph Roe attempt to escape
from the American federal prison on Alcatraz Island
in San Francisco Bay; neither is ever seen again.

DECEMBER 17

Today marks the 34th anniversary of the first flight of brothers
Wilbur and Orville Wright in Kill Devil Hills, North Carolina.

DECEMBER 18

Sixty Santa Claus impersonators, all of whom are members of the
Cleaners, Dyers, Pressers, Drivers, and Allied Trades Union, go on strike
from their moonlighting jobs as Santas in support of their union's strike.

DECEMBER 19

Four years ago today, Cicely Tyson was born
in Harlem, New York. She would become a
successful stage, screen, and television actress.
One of her earlier roles would be on the TV soap
opera *The Guiding Light,* which first aired
(as a radio program) in January of this year.

DECEMBER 20

Time magazine's cover for the week features Joseph
Stalin, superimposed over a blood-red map of Russia.

DECEMBER 21

Walt Disney's film *Snow White and the Seven Dwarfs,*
the first feature-length animated movie, is premiered
at the Carthay Circle Theater in Los Angeles.

DECEMBER 22

The Lincoln Tunnel opens to traffic in New York City.

DECEMBER 23

The Vickers Wellington bomber takes its first flight.

DECEMBER 24

Aviator, film producer, and business magnate
Howard Hughes celebrates his 32nd birthday.

DECEMBER 25

While the city around her celebrates Christmas, Sally Isley gives
birth to O'Kelly Isley Jr. in Cincinnati, Ohio. "Kelly" and his brothers
would found the legendary family group the Isley Brothers.

Mae West, shown here at the start of her Hollywood career, is losing popularity by 1937.
On December 12 she makes a guest appearance on NBC Radio's *Chase and Sanborn Hour;*
her lines and delivery are so risqué, she is banned from NBC stations.

DECEMBER 26

Jay B. Heimowitz, who would become
a celebrity poker player (earning more
than $2 million in live tournament
winnings), is born in Bethel, New York.

DECEMBER 27

Walt Disney is featured on the cover of *Time*
magazine, along with figurines of his Seven Dwarfs.

DECEMBER 28

Maurice Ravel (b. 1875), Swiss/French
composer *(Bolero),* dies in Paris at age 62.

DECEMBER 29

Pan Am airlines begins offering service
from San Francisco to Auckland, New Zealand.

DECEMBER 30

The consul general for Germany signs a contract in the Empire
State Building to participate in the New York World's Fair.

DECEMBER 31

Avram Hershko, future winner of the Nobel Prize
in Chemistry (2004), is born in Karcag, Hungary.

December finds the Congress of Industrial Organizations (CIO) on strike in the streets of
New York City.

The 1937 Shirley Temple film *Wee Willie Winkie* is a critical and box-office hit.

Pop Culture in
1937

Americans in 1937 needed fun pursuits to take their minds off the grim reality of life in economically uncertain times. One of the nation's favorite pastimes was going to the movies, and in 1937 the Hollywood movie industry was turning out a multitude of great entertainments. Walt Disney released the first feature-length animated film, *Snow White and the Seven Dwarfs*. Diminutive Shirley Temple continued to enchant the nation in *Heidi* and *Wee Willie Winkie*. The era of the screwball comedy was at its height, and films like *Nothing Sacred*, *Topper*, and *The Awful Truth* would go on to become beloved classics of the genre. Ronald Reagan, Lana Turner, and Glenn Ford made their cinematic debuts. Many of the greatest movie stars of all time appeared in films of 1937: Humphrey Bogart, Clark Gable, Cary Grant, Katharine Hepburn, Bette Davis, and Barbara Stanwyck are just a few. It was a glorious time to be going to the movies.

But there were plenty of other forms of entertainment to enjoy. Radio programs featured comedy, music, soap operas, and drama, with entertainers like Orson Welles, Rudy Vallee, and ventriloquist Edgar Bergen and his dummy, Charlie McCarthy. Bestselling novels included Margaret Mitchell's *Gone With the Wind*, published in June 1936 and still a nationwide hit. In sports, two guys named Joe (DiMaggio and Louis) captured the nation's attention. Americans of 1937 might have been struggling in many ways, but they were also blessed with an abundance of great entertainment.

A landmark for visitors and the focus of books, paintings, films, songs, and other cultural works, the Golden Gate Bridge (opened May 1937) is the symbol of San Francisco.

Top Five Male/Female Baby Names:

1. Robert/Mary
2. James/Barbara
3. John/Patricia
4. William/Shirley
5. Richard/Betty

***Publisher's Weekly*'s Best-Selling Novels of 1937:**

1. *Gone with the Wind* by Margaret Mitchell
2. *Northwest Passage* by Kenneth Roberts
3. *The Citadel* by A. J. Cronin
4. *And So—Victoria* by Vaughan Wilkins
5. *Drums Along the Mohawk* by Walter D. Edmonds

Top Five Highest-Grossing Movies:

1. *Snow White and the Seven Dwarfs*
2. *Saratoga*
3. *One Hundred Men and a Girl*
4. *Topper*
5. *Wee Willie Winkie*

Sports Champions:

U.S. Women's Figure Skating: Maribel Vinson
U.S. Men's Figure Skating: Robin Lee
Stanley Cup (hockey): Detroit Red Wings
America's Cup (yacht racing): *Ranger* (U.S.)
U.S. Women's Tennis: Anita Lizana
U.S. Men's Tennis: J.D. Budge
World Series: N.Y. Yankees
NFL football: Washington Redskins
Heavyweight Boxing: Joe Louis
Triple Crown (Thoroughbred racing): War Admiral
U.S. Open (golf): Ralph Guldahl
PGA golf: Denny Shute
Wimbledon women's singles tennis: Dorothy Round
Wimbledon gentlemen's singles tennis: Don Budge
Indianapolis 500: Wilbur Shaw
Heisman Trophy: Clint Frank (Yale, quarterback)
NAIA men's basketball (inaugural season): Central Missouri State

Luise Rainer stars in 1937's *The Good Earth,* for which she will take the Academy Award for Best Actress.

Final Associated Press Poll for College Football-Team Rankings:
1. Pittsburgh Panthers (9-0-1)
2. California Golden Bears (9-0-1)
3. Fordham Rams (7-0-1)
4. Alabama Crimson Tide (9-0)
5. Minnesota Golden Gophers (6-2)

Bowl Season:
Rose Bowl: #2 California Golden Bears vs. #4 Alabama Crimson Tide (13-0)
Sugar Bowl: #9 Santa Clara Broncos vs. #8 LSU Tigers (6-0)
Cotton Bowl: #18 Rice Owls vs. #17 Colorado Buffaloes (28-14)
Orange Bowl: Auburn Tigers vs. Michigan State Spartans (6-0)
Sun Bowl: West Virginia Mountaineers vs. Texas Tech Red Raiders (6-0)

Nobel Prizes:
Physics: Clinton Joseph Davisson and George Paget Thomson
Chemistry: Walter Norman Haworth; Paul Karrer
Physiology or Medicine: Albert von Szent-Györgyi Nagyrápolt
Literature: Roger Martin du Gard
Peace: Cecil of Chelwood, Viscount

Pulitzer Prizes
Public Service: *St. Louis Post-Dispatch*
Reporting: John J. O'Neill *(New York Herald Tribune)*; William L.
    Laurence *(New York Times)*; Howard W. Blakeslee (Associated
    Press); Gobind Behari Lal (Universal Service); and David Dietz
    (Scripps-Howard)
Correspondence: Anne O'Hare McCormick *(New York Times)*
Editorial Writing: John W. Owens *(Baltimore Sun)*
Editorial Cartooning: C. D. Batchelor *(New York Daily News)*
Novel: *Gone with the Wind* by Margaret Mitchell (Macmillan)
Drama: *You Can't Take It with You* by Moss Hart and
    George S. Kaufman (Farrar)
History: *The Flowering of New England 1815–1865* by
    Van Wyck Brooks (E.P. Dutton)
Biography or Autobiography: *Hamilton Fish* by Allan Nevins (Dodd)
Poetry: *A Further Range* by Robert Frost (Holt)

9th Academy Awards:
Best Picture: *The Great Ziegfeld*
Best Director: Frank Capra, *Mr. Deeds Goes to Town*

Future president Ronald Reagan is just getting his start as an actor. His first film, *Love Is on the Air,* is released October 2.

9th Academy Awards *(continued)*:
Best Actor: Paul Muni, *The Story of Louis Pasteur*
Best Actress: Luise Rainer, *The Great Ziegfeld*
Best Supporting Actor: Walter Brennan, *Come and Get It*
Best Supporting Actress: Gale Sondergaard, *Anthony Adverse*
Best Score: *Anthony Adverse*
Best Song: "The Way You Look Tonight," Swing Time

Notable Books Published:
Death on the Nile by Agatha Christie
The Hobbit by J.R.R. Tolkien
Of Mice and Men by John Steinbeck
To Have and Have Not by Ernest Hemingway

Top Songs of 1937:
Benny Goodman, "Sing, Sing, Sing"
Bing Crosby, "Sweet Leilani"
Count Basie, "One O'Clock Jump"
Fred Astaire, "They Can't Take That Away From Me"
Robert Johnson, "Hellhound on My Trail"

Five Commercial Food Products Introduced in 1937:
Hormel introduces Spam ("Spiced Ham"); 70 years later, the 7 billionth can of Spam would be sold.
The first Krispy Kreme doughnut is sold in Salem, North Carolina.
Kraft Dinner (later renamed Kraft Macaroni and Cheese) is introduced as "a meal for four in nine minutes for an everyday price of 19 cents."
Kix cereal is introduced by General Mills.
Pepperidge Farm commercial bakery is founded in 1937 by Margaret Rudkin, who got started by home-baking bread that her asthmatic son could safely eat, as he was allergic to most commercially processed foods.

Five Popular Radio Shows That Began in 1937:
The Edgar Bergen / Charlie McCarthy Show (1937–1956)
The Guiding Light (1937–1952)
The Shadow (1937–1954)
Mr. Keen, Tracer of Lost Persons (1937–1955)
The Tommy Dorsey Show (1937–1947)

Credits and Acknowledgments

Amandine Dupin wrote text; Holly Musgrove selected images. Individual image credits are as follows.

Chapter 1. George Takei—Beth Madison. Morgan Freeman—Georges Biard. Madeline Albright—U.S. Department of State. Richard Petty—Darryl Moran.

Chapter 2. Drug-store sign—Office of War Information. Federal Adult Schools—Federal Art Project, WPA. Store window—Russell Lee.

Chapter 3. Barbara Stanwyk—Studio publicity still. Lincoln Brigade memorial—Tom Hilton. Howard Hughes—Library of Congress. FDR's second inaugural address—Library of Congress. Scary scene—Torley. Tent in flood-refugee camp—Edwin Locke. General Colin Powell—John Clifton, U.S. Army. *Hindenburg*—U.S. Navy. Golden Gate Bridge opening—Prelinger Archives. Suburban Resettlement Administration poster—Bernanda Bryson, Suburban Resettlement Administration. Memorial Day massacre—National Archives. Jean Harlow—Harris & Ewing. *Peter Pan* movie poster—Paramount Pictures. Amelia Earhart—Wikimedia Commons. Tomb of the Unknown Soldier—John Collier. Man and liquor store—Arthur Rothstein. George Gershwin—George Grantham Bain Collection, Library of Congress. Camera—Nesster. Bessie Smith—Carl Van Vechten. Carthay Circle Theatre—*Los Angeles Times* photographic archive, UCLA Library. USS *Panay*—National Archives. Safety First poster—Allan Nase, artist for Works Projects Administration. Mae West—*New York World-Telegram & Sun*. CIO strikers—Arthur Rothstein.

Chapter 4. Shirley Temple—Harris & Ewing. Golden Gate Bridge—Brocken Inaglory. Luise Rainer—George Hurrell. Ronald Reagan—The Ronald Reagan Presidential Foundation and Library.